A Species of This Invaded World

For Pandelis & Julia,
"from straight to swinging"
yours,

ELIOT CARDINAUX

THE BODILY PRESS
Amherst, MA

A Species of This Invaded World

Copyright © 2025 Eliot Cardinaux

All rights reserved. Except for brief passages quoted
for usage in online or print sources (e.g. newspaper, magazine,
podcast), no part of this book may be reproduced in any form
or by any means, electronic or mechanical, including photocopying
and recording, or by any information storage and retrieval system,
without permission in writing from the publisher.

ISBN: 979-8-9988921-3-4

This book is set in Cardo, ITC Avant Garde Gothic Pro,
and Garamond Premier Pro.
Book design and layout by Eliot Cardinaux.
eliotcardinaux.com

Cover image:
Peter Knapp, *Sweet Peas*, 2021,
Woodcut, Edition of 10,
28"h x 20"w (71.1 x 50.8 cm).
All Rights Reserved.
Copyright © 2021 Peter Knapp

Bodily Press logo designed by Katya Popova.

THE BODILY PRESS
www.bodilypress.com
@thebodilypress

A Species of This
Invaded World
───────────────

Also by Eliot Cardinaux

POETRY

On the Long Blue Night
Quiet Labor
Toy Elegy
This Music From Another Room
The Ocean from Here to Here
Wandering Subject
Starlings

MUSIC

No Dreams Here
Gestures: Schaatsen (with Flin van Hemmen)
American Thicket (with Mat Maneri, Flin van Hemmen,
 & Thomas Morgan)
Sweet Beyond Witness
Magpie: Six Feet on Solid Ground (with Asger Thomsen
 & Jeppe Høi Justesen)
Odysseus Alone (with Kresten Osgood & Thomas Morgan)
Take Me By the Hand of Darkness (with Will McEvoy
 & Max Goldman)
A Living Past (with Jonas Engel, Asger Thomsen,
 & Simon Forchhammer)
What the Wildflower Witnessed (with Our Hearts as Thieves)
Pavane (with Gary Fieldman)
Out of Our Systems (with Will McEvoy & Max Goldman)
Pain is a Form of Violence Prone to Happiness
 (with Our Hearts as Thieves)
Imminence (with Gary Fieldman)
The Rock Beneath the Tree (with Bram Kincheloe)

for Tasha Robbins

You lived at zero, perhaps less, perhaps more.

—Mahmoud Darwish

The poem's hour of birth, ladies and gentlemen, lies in darkness. Some claim to know that it is the darkness just before dawn; I do not share this assumption.

—Paul Celan

this sky unexceptional at chess

—Bei Dao

Table of Contents

₼

I CARRY SOCIETY WITH ME

Mile Seventy-Two / 17
Mile Seventy-Three / 18
Mile Seventy-Four / 19

∴

XXVI. / 21
XXVII. / 22
XXVIII. / 23
XXIX. / 24
XXX. / 25

∴

Mile Seventy-Five / 28
Mile Seventy-Six / 29
Mile Seventy-Seven / 30

∴

XXXI. / 32
XXXII. / 34
XXXIII. / 35
XXXIV. / 36
XXXV. / 38

∴

Mile Seventy-Eight / 41
Mile Seventy-Nine / 42
Mile Eighty / 43

⁞

XXXVI. / 45
XXXVII. / 46
XXXVIII. / 47
XXXIX. / 48
XL. / 49

∴

Mile Eighty-One / 51
Mile Eighty-Two / 52
Mile Eighty-Three / 53

♇

bombs / 59

FOOTPRINTS

Mile Eighty-Four / 79
Mile Eighty-Five / 80
Mile Eighty-Six / 81
Mile Eighty-Seven / 82
Mile Eighty-Eight / 83

❖

XLI. / 85
XLII. / 86
XLIII. / 87
XLIV. / 88
XLV. / 89

⁂

Mile Eighty-Nine / 91
Mile Ninety / 92
Mile Ninety-One / 93
Mile Ninety-Two / 94
Mile Ninety-Three / 95
Mile Ninety-Four / 96
Mile Ninety-Five / 97

❖

XLVI. / 99
XLVII. / 100
XLVIII. / 101
XLIX. / 102
L. / 103

⁜

Mile Ninety-Six / 105
Mile Ninety-Seven / 106
Mile Ninety-Eight / 107
Mile Ninety-Nine / 108
Mile One-Hundred / 109

₱

Acknowledgments / 113

Notes / 115

About the Author / 123

I CARRY SOCIETY WITH ME

∴

Mile Seventy-Two

Crocus, fleeting
antidote to history,

recognize the sadness
already there.

Mile Seventy-Three

Brief grace, the
limits of my body

tragically tied to
the face of things.

An old, ineffect-
ual creeping.

Dazed & now-
here. Ripe for

disregard. Man-
dated safely to

parrot assumed
consent.

Mile Seventy-Four

A cycle. Expression.
Failure. Hand in

hand. A matter
of marking the way.

Onward & inward,
one might say,

& through
this

learn
to be lonely.

If only a song
were heard.

XXVI.

for Ian Fishman

it is raining in the sunlight   hope is the thing
tarred & feathered   in the street   & a lot is
changing   begin to recover   birds overhead
whistle agitated laughter   my mantra
I spy a love in the window

a species of this   invaded world I want no more
the unbroken   singular   voice to bend my will with
the unseeing eye of this silence   human yet
to hold the endgame

that was not a bot   that was Michael Palmer
putting pressure on memory to remind itself
of air   from the underground springs
beneath   Walter Benjamin's Berlin
es sind noch Lieder zu singen   jenseits
der Menschen   a more-than-human
thing

you   tripping publisher   mobbed by a murder
of crows   I remember   alien music in the Vondelpark
too   as marketed to hippies   on <u>ufodrum.com</u>
good content for a *cursèd place*

XXVII.

not broken   not breaking   ever
on the cusp of disaster   radiant
miles grow longer   the days   stand in for
a question   sun marks the way like a stone

easy does it   trying my best to live this
every stone unturned   leaves a thriving
habitat alone   can it be said   that to listen
is to have written the book

hallelujah   sacred music
some kind of documentary
gives birth to the open air
the world as surely

XXVIII.

for Catherine Corbett Bresner

locus of virtue   from which
we are exempt   now   I must douse myself
in sleep   the rhythm   the rhythm
toys with my breath   I sing
to bathe in the question   is to speak
an answer

tiptoe lightly on my tongue   the words
are searing   what does it make me
answer *nothing*   the excess becoming
a catalog   pollen in the air   the leaves
are green now   poised for the open road
down South   do things move
more slowly still

sleep cycles   time zones   site
of a waking dream   to craft
mythology   out of a bedtime story
basketball streaming   down my cheeks
like a sudden claw   a ring through which things
are birthed   in public
litters

XXIX.

for Nicole Peyrafitte

another   fitting tributary
madness to the methodology
a Baltimore fox   is it playing
is it searching for nests
in the bushes   to suck the eggs

so close it came to us
& stared us down with a grin
as if to alleviate   panic
outside our dishonest
liminal abode

beauty again keeps the whole
world whole   hygienic
towels   a sparrow on a bed
of oyster crackers   Poultney
& Panapsco   scrap   *what will
you make of it*   a negative
three glue sticks   a piece
of checkered paper   black
foam   five dollars in a little bag

XXX.

for & with Shana Bulhan

Tuesday at the laundromat
a woman injured
in the subjunctive
half-singing   half-cooing
as if fawning over a cat
who isn't there

last night in the car
debating the various uses
of the word *independence:*
the ability to pay another
to do things for you   therefore
dependence

or the ability
to do everything oneself:
the unreachable
individual ideal

therefore the assumption
of the many   fawning over each
en masse
the spectre of applause

energy dominance   is
national security

thinking through the poem
I wonder   what is the cat's
name

∴

Mile Seventy-Five

Sides of broad daylight,
a signal, white as snow

has hampered you, brought
news of your doings there.

Zero, your future, bright
signal from nowhere, burns.

Mile Seventy-Six

*for David Need,
i.m. Alice Notley*

Applaud me, wan-
dering & failing this

shared wilderness,
if only for a night.

Those dreams were
fluid & unsettling.

How can I change
it? Catch up with

thought as I rediscover
the poem, holding

the book in my hand.
Small place, there, for

memory, finding one-
self on stage, in shock.

Mile Seventy-Seven

Go far. Go further
in reverse. Experience

the maniac inter-
ruption of art, un-

fed. Hang the work
in this space. Charge

the admission of doubt
in the mourning. Coffee.

Grime. Cement. Official
inaction, read *engagement*.

Aid, read *ammunition*.
Loss, *red death & murder*.

❖

XXXI.

i.m. Daniel Levine

not so far from the edge
I am haunted by ghost cries
yours   from across the hall
a right-wing pundit laughing
from a neighbor's studio
the echo of birdsong trapped
underneath the canopy
rainwater's reverb   a distant
siren   cars rushing by
quotidian   the wind

I light a cigarette
inside the bookstore
practicing social ecology
I dream a little to the left
of the speaker's inertia
static of an era   gathers
like a symphony   a storm
takes its sweet time
diagnosing cataracts

to study alongside
quilt societies   the gossips
dismantle a ladder across
the way   the laws inverted
by human agency
break open the ocean

a sigh of relief to witness
the living practicum
text & *hors-texte*   jettison
whole classes of people
out of the territory
into a common world

XXXII.

*for & with Jo Ianni,
i.m. Alice Notley*

I wouldn't trust the meat
off the hunter's bone   lost
in the Pentagon parking lot
Baltimore fox says
do not worry   & indeed
I worry a lot about this life
& everything   everyone
at its edge

sour the hunter's stomach
create some distance   let
the flowers grow   be vegan
if you want   humanity is not
delicious   neither
to be done away with
milk it for what it's worth

seasons   salt of the earth
& the spice of death   the price
of dust   to run on & on   though
I am not soluble   in unbottled water
to market the filtered ocean
unlike me

XXXIII.

for Deja Rene Carr

relaxing is the hardest
work   each phrase
contradicting the last
frantically relaxing   that is
the only task of madness
domestic & classical
as it is

talking to a spider outside
the outpatient unit   maybe
they will understand
death's statistics   not to excuse
the president   for the difficult
position he's in

it is love that reveals
the injustices   never silence
the critic   address the source
I am speaking to the center
of a void without words
leave my meaning   by
the wayside   take
what sound you can
more music
for the public square

XXXIV.

for Michael Palmer

what is a house or a home
visibility throttles   disembodied
brains   the scum of the earth
wished well   turns out
if you rip someone's
heart out   & devour it
like a maniac   they'll die

keep asking for money
do the right thing   amphibian
under lilypads   to strategize
transcendence as a means
eye to eye   oblivion
till the shoulder meets
the heart   in the lion's
mouth   an oeuvre
outside the text
will you fawn
or throttle me

Johnny Appleseed
buried the town
buried the village
buried   the encampment
buried the landscape under fire
buried the apple   once
& for all   in Adam's
throat   Europe
sings   *vos rêves*
un peu fervents

XXXV.

for & with Shana Bulhan

to tell the tale of this
love of mine   they were
a thousand glorious
little cats   black sheep
the undefined *carte blanche*
of a body   outside the systemic
structure   on which
this is written   in
white ink:

nothing is possible
at last   ending a months-
long search for disappearance
the difference between us
growing like a sieve

if all the exhaustion
has led us here   nowhere
together we can speak
everything at once
commit the acts in layers
over the mind

nothing is
possible   we'll do it now
that the thorny zero
has sprung its rose

∴

Mile Seventy-Eight

for Patrick Pritchett

Long fall from the edge
of absolution, admission

is not such a costly thing.
To have searched for this

long, no wavering. I see
the interpellation gather

seasons under its wing.
White hair, white throat,

white word, then nothing.
The origin of a prayer.

Mile Seventy-Nine

for Shana Bulhan

You are
magnificent

& usher in
a new era

of beautiful
dawns. So that

they know,
there are also

good things
like this.

Mile Eighty

Raise a bruise
the colors of

loud memory.
Honor the fickle

fire of each pre-
ceding term.

Do we march
again to heighten

the festivities
of a year-long

age? Born
just after

the war, the
place itself

will be a lie,
no longer there,

more map
than insistence.

⁘

XXXVI.

for paul catafago

in times like these
your kind words mean the world
rushing into the room   a fool
of me & you   between all
relations   *persona non
grata*   meaning absence
referring to every wounded
sincerity

to go into lapping water   eye
to eye   a sadness   not to be washed
off   discarded stones   an archipelago
of stars   where salt rims the edges
of a book   so much   space
in the margins   swimming
on land over sky   blue water
sex   bleeding over the world

these mourning movements
stasis   what it's like to live with
fear of being shaken off   *intifada*
medusa   traipsing the garden path
a diminutive largeness   real
tears   brought the bright
hazy day   into view
too late   for the absolute

XXXVII.

i.m. Daniel Levine

Beatrice bones of the trumpet
hall of mirrors   a house
with many names   'Round Midnight
beautiful *fuck you*   to get inside
the thing & not   to turn away

not knowing   who one is
in relation to a room
where Dante & Sam Rivers
leap from junk to junk
before the threat of God
from flame   to imitation
a human word

the mundanity of a piano
on the other side of the room
slam a hand down
on the table   knowing
it is not yours

XXXVIII.

for Niamh Timmons

I have a hunch
my head is in the bushes
shadow all around   behind me
a forked branch   the backdrop
just minutes before   of a silent scream
hands pouring down
like pressure   surrounding
a joyous face

to gain a little space
push your elbows out
disappointing all
expectations of youth

a dead snake in the attic   neglected
along with the other trash   to stand before
what court   how very radical   people
fool themselves   like this

XXXIX.

for mireille gansel

the poem comes
while waiting for my head
to clear   three days now
staring at a wall of disaster
work willing to be done
pro bono   I cannot complain
only fear

the worst every day   to get up
in spite of it   be diligent
slipping   out of synch
with whatever mission
yours   mine   the others'
across the way   across land
& sea   & river   helping
the word to pass

I carry in my mouth a home
for this language   I carry
a mouse that lives there
the cat who hunts her
for the people who stray
from the shores of my tongue
the tip of it always
in need   of meaning

XL.

for Karen Haydock

everything here is extra large
can no longer afford itself
the courtesy of a gesture
to speak of cathexis again
here I am   & I want to talk
about you

good things stream in
shut out   disaster   mother
of my love   bringing aloo
chole   *how could the English
need spices   if they don't know
the meaning*   a cadenza
is what this is

∴

Mile Eighty-One

Small wonder,
the uniform being

your disguise. In-
filtration wills us

to collapse. Why
murder, from straight

to swinging, first
person, then plural,

as reason dictates?
The way is clear.

Mile Eighty-Two

To stare down
this absence,

asking the heart
be ruled. All bitter

breaking of
the light. Imagine

the Atlantic. Frail
the white rose, as

dawn comes dancing
over the bay.

Mile Eighty-Three

Territorial flourish.
The land sprawls

newly under a map
of burning

trees. Settled,
the world resorts

to reformulation.
Dead air lengthens

the eerie street
dancing out in it-

self, repeating, day
after day.

bombs

bombs

the light from our eyes drifts further into space.
to distract the sun. its longest sojourn in the sky.
if light can see what you see on your deathbed.

bombs

we are asking. after. your menacing
laughter. so we are told. it couldn't be.
couldn't be enough. most people.
most people wouldn't say.

bombs

this might be the start of another.
where you & I end. whom to speak
& to speak to. target which address.

bombs

the sun is an empty tunnel. withdrawal blast open. clutter of pitches. sleep cells huddle around a bright, rich chord.

bombs

who said the world is the asylum.
I can't remember. dying. so it must
be real. the greatest objects. serve
a body's function. creep your way.

bombs

reality lies. because you say.
to hour the inconceivable.
how you take. your word.
when excess is all we have.

bombs

desire gives in on itself. the honeyed light.
your weight at the window. bodies sprawled
across a page. dejected siblings. heavy
tender. sun and heat.

bombs

cool air. glass cathedral.
drunk myself dry. cloud
cover of a book fallen
into. lie at base level now.

bombs

rim of my crater. self-insufficient.
moreover. detonate your pride.
limning the middle gender.
the earth resists like you.

bombs

to reach across. great space.
that is. the page. an ocean
links the worst of us. states
open onto actions. speech.

bombs

divest of this. don't use those words
here. anyone said. anyone did. these
things. anyone might have. anyone
could be underground before now.

bombs

suffer. waiting for this to be over.
asking what solution there is. over
land and water. stolen away. gone
goodness. asking for land over sea.

bombs

sad. that I want the world to end
so we can sleep again. is that how
you feel. this will all be over soon.
tomorrow comes for some people.

bombs

reluctant hopeful. tease and be teased. struggle with that. stick your head in the freezer. make yourself cooler. bittersweet.

bombs

what can you do. about
what happened. you can
wish it had happened to
you. come to think it did.

bombs

stop. but not before
you chant freedom.
running for office.
running from you.

bombs

imperfect world. you are unideal.
as me. unideal as this. or art. maybe
art is unideal. the ideal itself. what
excludes you from your utopia.

FOOTPRINTS

DOMINANCE

Mile Eighty-Four

i.m. Fanny Howe

Broken in
the sense

that paradise
is always

troubled,
childhood

climbs this
place of

tranquil
water,

swings
from the

short north-
ern lights.

Mile Eighty-Five

Listen,
to steady

the glare of
your silent

double, with-
holding

your own no-
madness.

What is ex-
pected but not

allowed.
Due labor

& limit-
ation. To

try &
tribulate.

Mile Eighty-Six

Invader, needling, as if
the sea were prophecy,

riding the metal wave,
you are kept from meaning,

searching for water
the color of birdsong,

alert but not alert
to pain.

Mile Eighty-Seven

Mile, mirror,
ordinance,

each season
in its cell.

An awful
time, but

we are alive,
which is why

it hurts. The
work feels

empty. I love
you still.

Mile Eighty-Eight

Become small
in the time

that is lost, here,
grieving your

exile, homeless
creature, wan-

ting so desperate-
ly to return.

⁘

XLI.

rainbow over home   gone rainbow
over Shana in the window   the power
back on   under condition of circumstance
symptom of mystery   manipulation
double edge of beauty   seeing
what's not there   your life on the lawn

so tender   tender   gentle scrape of claws
down my midriff   metal on tension
near tears   ban my shadow   in this
least real of worlds

there will always be more you can do
to ignite   your agency   this is how
fire works   burn brightly   burn
for eight days   better not
burn out

XLII.

they are coming up the mountain
how else can she drive   six white
horses   how can she sing   *hallelujah*
chariots of fire   laying waste to the land
of the prophets   suicidal impulse
open the closet door

name not the thing but the thing's
existence   candle-bright   & full
of hunger   going out at night
to count the years   draw no map
& quarter   this ripening
century

soon you'll be skipping stones   you'll see
on the border   between   this dedication
& that   identity   gone lost   gone very quiet
indeed   if rage is a wall   *a river*
flows through your notebook   don't
you misspell its name

XLIII.

for Shana Bulhan

o cat of mine   I will pet you ferociously
& without relent   no matter what
falls from the sky

I have tried to enclose
the rhetoric of maps
in what summer calls
a flower   why do I have
to explain

the origin
of music   water
dripping on a leaf
if gravity is tied
to grace

XLIV.

for Tasha Robbins

put it in the river   twelve
miles to go   to whose destination
how many tons of explosives   your trauma
now mine   to grieve   what species
twists out of this trellis
onto the world

it's not that I don't see valence
desire in its distant softness
to live outside the law
you have to be honest
what does it really mean

to cultivate a landscape
speak of transference
& care   the way we labor
welcome to the world   infer
our friendship   take no money
& run   it can go   both ways
for hours on the phone

XLV.

when poets go into hiding
will I be hunted   or hunting
myself   still waiting on the cost
of living   to validate the pain
you have to feel it   deeply I sing
to you   *you've changed*

to locate the speaker
beyond the veil   *in the rivers*
north of the future   tesseractic
landscape   gone sparkle
in your eye as witness
to go on living

Mile Eighty-Nine

*Aesthetics thus
demands hiddenness*

*and rewards it,
ethics demands*

*disclosure and
punishes hiddenness.*

Today is upon us.
Hunger, there is

no waking to what
is concealed.

Mile Ninety

for Niamh Timmons

It is not your fault
that things become

so small. Immobile,
tasked to wait, &

covet your hospital
bed. As if it existed

as right & possession,
in need of making.

Mile Ninety-One

Small nightmare,
do not compare

yourself to willful
tragedy. Pots & pans

are sounding in
the public square

against a hunger
greater than any

blockade. Why is it
music to my ears?

Mile Ninety-Two

Year of the body,
year of continued

death, what is it
like to cry out

in surprise at this
juncture, priming

an indigenous
palimpsest

if this is what
you've made.

Mile Ninety-Three

for Mark Scroggins

Contemporaneity.
The long, slow crash

& heave of time
on the shores

of history. Why
there is fashion

on crowded streets
& orders to round

up the people who
live there for lack

of shelter. These,
the true cities.

Mile Ninety-Four

The air clears
as people spill

onto the bus. I
write you, to-

ward ascension,
into view.

Mile Ninety-Five

There is no end,
dead flower. Open

onto the insanity
of numbers. Try

again. Reach out
to power with a

spell, the tendrils of
which are your eyes.

XLVI.

blood on the knife
blade   the handle
in the snow   your
own tongue unspeaks
your name

but don't be so sure
how I feel   or what
I think of you   *canis
lupus*   hunted in the name
of protection

though there might be
some distance between us
how can that be
subjective

XLVII.

for Uche Nduka

in the way a crab is useful
scuttle the English language
meridians   latch onto native
landscapes   into the terrarium
of Earth   the submarine human
heart braids its way   across your face
pausing   at each station of the word
to drink of itself   eat of itself
brain   ghost   & paradise

at which point   lost meaning
accrual   dance   & consequence
move along serial lines   as miles
give way   to numeral

XLVIII.

for Adam Stutz

tricky landing to stick between fact
& connotation   failure is a way of saying
I tried   but don't be   too afraid
of the Florida gulag   it means
amusement park   to those
who have vied & failed
historically   for labor

this is what was said
no wonder mushrooms
thread the zeitgeist with
possibility   futureless
& intact   as yet

a human culture
fails to project itself
stats & options   bonds
onto success or succession
the linear nightmare

er ruft stecht tiefer ins Erdreich
ihr einen   er ruft spielt süßer
den Tod   death
is a master
from anywhere

XLIX.

for Shana & Niamh

we are living   despite the madness
there is a place for highway music
still   in the folds of the big blue sky
like a blast of hot air   to the face
& history   unrelenting   brings nothing
new

it's just that we can see it
can't avoid it   coming now
to terms with annulled agreement
the windows down in our minds
carefree   despite the impossible
objects   on the road to equation
spikes   in the tiring curve of it

L.

for David Need

as you said   there is no wilderness
I carry society with me   my friend
had plans to be here   maybe he had
the last laugh   it's getting so hard
to tell what death means   political
action   trouble   all around

what if I plead with you   cover
all spiritual bases   *do not hurt*
one another   please   be cautious
the world is fraught with danger
we deserve each other at least

but I do not find   that cynical mentality
to exist among strangers   take away
the stakes   admit   reality as it is
we are in the streets because of hunger
hunger is in the streets

Mile Ninety-Six

Zone of slow
unraveling,

I have to
water the poor,

dejected
basil.

Mile Ninety-Seven

for Dana Henry Martin

That was the year
that madness came

to stay. Not on our
couch per se. To

all of us. &
madness is

no horror. Is it
at its height or

at its end? A long
road to tentative

disappearance. I
can see you, mad-

ness. Can you see
me? Peek-a-boo,

madness,
peek-a-boo.

Mile Ninety-Eight

To sour the human
experience, the human

in humanity boils
to a bridge. Harmonic.

Walking the hills
as King Lear.

Mile Ninety-Nine

O to be a cat
to be a cat

to be
a cat

Mile One-Hundred

Road so long
it dangles from

the sky above
the city like

a note blaring
day. If the world

were perfect there
would be no need.

Acknowledgments

"Mile Eighty" first appeared in a journal curated by Shistri Sainani for Ahmedabad Art Week (India). My thanks for the inclusion.

"XLII" first appeared in *Cataloguing Poetry Magazine*. My thanks to the editor, John Compton.

Thank you to all those who have supported my work as a poet and publisher with The Bodily Press this past year, in larger and smaller ways. This book, and many others like it, are made possible by your consistent readership and commitment to the art of poetry and the small press.

Thanks also to the authors I publish, whose work seeps into everything I do, transforming the landscape of my own life and poetry for the better.

Thank you to Daniel Levin at Sanctuary Series for inviting me down to Durham, North Carolina to perform my piece "Black Swans," and for believing in my music at least as much as my poetry.

Thank you to Ellen Miller-Mack for providing an outlet for me and the authors I publish on the Poet Talk podcast (Spotify/ WMUA 91.1 FM Amherst, MA).

Thank you to Tasha Robbins for helping me *put it in the river*.

Thank you to Peter Knapp for the generous use of his beautiful woodcut.

Thank you to Uche Nduka and David Need for being such attuned first readers of this work.

Thank you to Niamh Timmons for remaining a streadfast friend through thick and thin.

A final, special thank you to my life partner Shana Bulhan, whose keen editorial eyes and ears are outmatched only by their rare abundance of empathy and sincerity in the face of a common, burning world.

Notes

epigraphs:

Mahmoud Darwish, *In the Presence of Absence* (pg. 49), Sinan Antoon, translator (NYRB, 2012).

Paul Celan, *Microliths They Are, Little Stones: Posthumous Prose* (pg. 132), Pierre Joris, translator (Contra Mundum Press, 2020).

Bei Dao, "Another," *At the Sky's Edge: Poems 1991-1996* (pg. 95), David Hinton and Yanbing Chen, translators (New Directions, 2001).

pg. 21

es sind noch Lieder zu singen jenseits der Menschen: "there are still songs to sing beyond [human]kind." Paul Celan, *"Fadensonnen"* / "Threadsuns," *Breathturn into Timestead: The Collected Later Poetry* (pg. 14), Pierre Joris, translator (FSG 2014).

pg. 26

energy dominance is national security: billboard glimpsed from the highway in Washington D.C.

pg. 33

a common world: the title of a book by Andrew Mossin (Bodily Press, 2025).

pg. 35

> *never silence the critic address the source:* Paul Robeson: "The answer to injustice is not to silence the critic, but to end the injustice."

pg. 36-37

> *till the shoulder meets the heart:* "*Jusqu'au coup d'épaule en plein cœur*" René Char, "*La Rose Violente*" | "The Violent Rose," *Le Marteau sans maître* | *The Hammer Without a Master* (J. Corti, 1954), transl. Eliot Cardinaux.

> *vos rêves un peu fervents:* "your slightly fervent dreams," mireille gansel, from her introduction to *Arsenal & Other Poems*, René Char, Eliot Cardinaux, translator (Bodily Press, forthcoming). "I'd come all the way to this haven of clarity [(René Char's home)], to bring to him from Hanoi, then devastated by the B52 bombs, the dream that the poet Tê Hanh entrusted to me, yes his slightly crazy, slightly fervent dream, to translate him into Vietnamese …" See also gansel, *Translation as Transhumance* (Feminist Press at CUNY, 2017), pg. 73-76.

pg. 46

> *Dante & Sam Rivers:* hear Sam Rivers, "Beatrice," *Fuchsia Swing Song* (Blue Note, 1965).

> *leap from junk to junk:* Osip Mandelstam, "Conversation About Dante," Clarence Brown and Robert Hughes, translators, *The Selected Poems of Osip Mandelstam* (NYRB, 2004): "One has to run across the whole width

of the river, jammed with mobile Chinese junks sailing in various directions. This is how the meaning of poetic speech is created. Its route cannot be reconstructed by interrogating the boatmen: they will not tell how and why we were leaping from junk to junk" (pg. 105).

pg. 52

Frail the white rose: James Joyce, "A Flower Given to My Daughter," *Poems Pennyeach* (Shakespeare and Co., 1927), pg. 3.

pg. 59-75

the short serial poem "**bombs**" was written during the so-called "Twelve-Day War" begun on June 13th 2025, when Israel bombed Iranian nuclear sites unprovoked during negotiations to broker an Iranian nuclear deal.

pg. 79

the short northern lights: Fanny Howe, "[I won't be able to write from the grave]," *Selected Poems* (University of California Press, 2000), pg. 204.

pg. 81

riding the metal wave, / you are kept from meaning, // searching for water / the color of birdsong: after Mahmoud Darwish, from *Memory for Forgetfulness* (University of California Press, 1995), Ibrahim Muhawi, translator. Written in besieged Beirut in 1982: "The dawn made of lead is still advancing from the direction of the sea, riding on sounds I haven't heard before. The sea has been entirely packed into stray shells. It is changing its marine nature and turning into metal. Does death have all these names? [...] Water under these conditions comes to us like a miracle. Who says water has no color, flavor, or smell? Water does have a color that reveals itself in the unfolding of thirst. Water has the color of bird sounds, that of sparrows in particular—birds that pay no heed to this war approaching from the sea" (pg. 9-10).

pg. 86

name not the thing but the thing's / existence: Osip Mandelstam, "The Morning of Acmeism," *Complete Critical Prose,* Jane Gary Harris and Constance Link, translators (Ardis, 1979): "Love the existence of the thing more than the thing itself and your own existence more than yourself" (pg. 42).

candle-bright / & full / of hunger: Paul Celan, "By the undreamt" | "*Von Ungeträumten,*" "a place, through which I / can wake myself toward you, / the bright / hunger-candle in mouth." *Breathturn into Timestead* (pg. 3).

a river flows through your notebook: Mahmoud Darwish, *In the Presence of Absence,* Sinan Antoon, translator (NYRB, 2012): "The world is gradually born out of words. [...] If you do not misspell "river," the river will flow through your notebook" (pg. 28).

pg. 88

put it in the river: a saying in New Orleans for letting things go, i.e. into the Mississippi.

to live outside the law / you have to be honest: Bob Dylan, paraphrased from "Absolutely Sweet Marie," *Blonde On Blonde* (Columbia Records, 1966): "To live outside the law / you must be honest."

pg. 89

gone sparkle / in your eye: a riff off the song "You've Changed," Carl Fischer, music; Bill Carey, lyrics (1942), recorded by Billie Holiday on *Lady In Satin* (Columbia, 1958).

to locate the speaker / beyond the veil: see Fred Moten's essay on Holiday, "The Dark Lady and the Sexual Cut," from *In the Break* (University of Minnesota Press, 2003): "the ghostly emanation of those last records, the sound that extends beyond the end of which it tells" (pg. 119).

in the rivers north of the future: "... I cast the net, which you / hesitantly weight / with shadows stones / wrote." Paul Celan, *Breathturn into Timestead* (pg. 5).

pg. 91

Aesthetics thus demands hiddenness and rewards it, ethics demands disclosure and punishes hiddenness: Paul Celan, *Microliths* (pg. 88).

pg. 99

blood on the knife blade / the handle in the snow / your own tongue unspeaks your name: in reference to the song "Wolves," by Dead Prez, from the album *Let's Get Free* (Loud Records, 2000), which features an excerpt of a speech Chairman Omali Yeshitela gave to the Black Power Organizing Conference in Philadelphia on May 31st, 1998.

pg. 100

in the way a crab is useful: James Baldwin, "The Artist's Struggle for Integrity," from *The Cross of Redemption: Uncollected Writings* (Knopf Doubleday, 2010): "Most people live in almost total darkness…people, millions of people whom you will never see, who don't know you, never will know you, people who may try to kill you in the morning, live in a darkness which…if you have that funny terrible thing which every artist can recognize and no artist can define…you are responsible to those people to lighten, and it does not matter what happens to you. You are being used in the way a crab is useful, the way sand certainly has some function. It is impersonal" (pg. 55).

pausing / at each station of the word: in *A Nomad Poetics* (Wesleyan University Press, 2003), Pierre Joris writes repeatedly about the concept of "mawqif," an Arabic word whose meaning he describes as "the pause, the stop-over, the rest, the stay of the wanderer between two moments of movement, two runs, two sites, two places, two states" (pg. 47). This and other concepts in *A Nomad Poetics* greatly inform the construction of the two long serial poems featured in this collection.

pg. 101

er ruft stecht tiefer ins Erdreich ihr einen / er ruft spielt süßer den Tod: "He calls out jab deeper into the earth you there / ... / He calls out play death more sweetly [death is a master from Deutschland]" ... Paul Celan, from "*Todesfuge,*" | "Deathfugue," as collected in *Memory Rose into Threshold Speech: The Collected Earier Poetry* (pg. 42-45), Pierre Joris, translator (FSG, 2020).

pg. 103

there is no wilderness: David Need, "Buddhist Meditation Blues," *Broken Windows* (Bodily Press, 2025), pg. 52.

About the Author

ELIOT CARDINAUX is a poet, pianist, composer, publisher, and translator working at the edges of the lyric and improvised music. The author of *On the Long Blue Night* (Dos Madres, 2023), *Quiet Labor*, *Toy Elegy*, *This Music From Another Room* (Bodily Press, 2024), *The Ocean from Here to Here*, *Wandering Subject*, and *Starlings* (Bodily Press, 2025), as well as numerous chapbooks, Eliot has also produced and appeared on over a dozen albums of original music, including *American Thicket* (Loyal Label, 2016), *Out of Our Systems*, *Pavane* (Bodily Press, 2022), and most recently *Imminence* (self-released, 2024) with drummer/percussionist Gary Fieldman. They hold a bachelor's degree in contemporary improvisation from The New England Conservatory of Music, and an MFA in creative writing, with a focus on poetry, from the University of Massachusetts in Amherst. Eliot's poems and translations have appeared in *Jacket2*, *Meridian*, *Spoon River Poetry Review*, *Bennington Review*, *Tupelo Quarterly*, *California Quarterly*, *The Arts Fuse*, *Solstice*, and elsewhere. At present, they co-lead a trio with bassist Will McEvoy and drummer Max Goldman. Eliot performs throughout Europe and the Northeast United States. They have taught literature and writing at UMass Amherst, and music as a postgraduate mentor at the Copenhagen Rhythmic Music Conservatory in Denmark. They work as a bookseller at Amherst Books. They are also the founding editor of The Bodily Press, through which they have published books and chapbooks by Nathaniel Mackey, Patrick Pritchett, Sarah Menefee, Deja Rene Carr (AKA Mal Devisa), John Phillips, Tasha Robbins, Mark Scroggins, and others.

Author photograph by poet Shana Bulhan ⨎ shanabulhan.com

THE BODILY PRESS
bodilypress.bandcamp.com
www.bodilypress.com
@thebodilypress